Beatrix Potter

Jennifer Hurtig

www.av2books.com

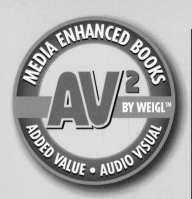

AV² provides enriched content that supplements and complements this book. Weigl's AV² books strive to create inspired learning and engage young minds in a total learning experience.

Your AV² Media Enhanced books come alive with...

Audio
Listen to sections of the book read aloud.

Key Words
Study vocabulary, and complete a matching word activity.

Video
Watch informative video clips.

Quizzes
Test your knowledge.

Go to **www.av2books.com**, and enter this book's unique code.

Embedded Weblinks
Gain additional information for research.

Slide Show
View images and captions, and prepare a presentation.

BOOK CODE

X 6 2 2 2 6 8

AV² by Weigl brings you media enhanced books that support active learning.

Try This!
Complete activities and hands-on experiments.

... and much, much more!

Published by AV² by Weigl
350 5th Avenue, 59th Floor
New York, NY 10118

Website: www.weigl.com www.av2books.com

Library of Congress Cataloging-in-Publication Data

Hurtig, Jennifer.
 Beatrix Potter / Jennifer Hurtig.
    pages cm. -- (Remarkable Writers)
 Includes index.
 Summary: "Part of a biography series that profiles children's authors of the twentieth century. Explores the life of Beatrix Potter and her most popular books, with additional facts provided through a timeline, awards, and fan information. Includes photographs, creative writing tips, and instruction on how to write a biography report. Intended for fourth to sixth grade students"--Provided by publisher.
 ISBN 978-1-62127-402-5 (hardcover : alk. paper) -- ISBN 978-1-62127-408-7 (softcover : alk. paper)
 1. Potter, Beatrix, 1866-1943--Juvenile literature. 2. Authors, English--20th century--Biography--Juvenile literature. 3. Artists--Great Britain--Biography--Juvenile literature. 4. Children's stories--Authorship--Juvenile literature. I. Title.
 PR6031.O72Z5875 2014
 823'.912--dc23
 [B]
                         2012040799

Printed in the United States of America, in North Mankato, Minnesota
1 2 3 4 5 6 7 8 9 0 17 16 15 14 13

012013
WEP301112

Senior Editor: Heather Kissock
Design: Terry Paulhus

Weigl acknowledges Getty Images as its primary photo supplier for this title.

Contents

Introducing Beatrix Potter

Beatrix Potter created some of the most beloved books of all time, including *The Tale of Peter Rabbit*. Beatrix's books take readers on a wonderful journey into the make-believe world of mischief-making, talking animals.

As a child, Beatrix did not have many friends, so she spent most of her time reading, studying, drawing, and writing. She wrote stories and drew pictures of her pets, as well as animals she saw on farms and in the countryside.

Over time, Beatrix's friends and family encouraged her to share her stories with the world. She looked for ways to publish her work, finding success in the early 1900s. For years, Beatrix wrote and illustrated many tales about whimsical animals. Children all over the world enjoyed reading her books, and young readers continue to cherish these stories.

📖 Children often get an early introduction to Beatrix Potter and her book characters.

Writing A
Biography

Writers are often inspired to record the stories of people who lead interesting lives. The story of another person's life is called a biography. A biography can tell the story of any person, from authors such as Beatrix Potter, to inventors, presidents, and sports stars.

When writing a biography, authors must first collect information about their subject. This information may come from a book about the person's life, a news article about one of his or her accomplishments, or a review of his or her work. Libraries and the internet will have much of this information. Most biographers will also interview their subjects. Personal accounts provide a great deal of information and a unique point of view. When some basic details about the person's life have been collected, it is time to begin writing a biography.

As you read about Beatrix Potter, you will be introduced to the important parts of a biography. Use these tips and the examples provided to learn how to write about an author or any other remarkable person.

📖 Beatrix Potter's imaginative stories have made her one of the bestselling children's authors of all time.

Today, Beatrix Potter's original drawings are kept in museums and galleries. Movies, a ballet, and stage shows have been made about her life. Her timeless stories have been enjoyed by people everywhere.

Early Life

Helen Beatrix Potter was born on July 28, 1866, in London, England. Her father was a wealthy lawyer. Beatrix's parents were busy with work and other activities, so Beatrix was raised mainly by servants and **governesses**.

"Thank goodness I was never sent to school; it would have rubbed off some of the originality."
—*Beatrix Potter*

When Beatrix was six years old, her brother Bertram was born. Bertram went away to boarding school when he was 11 and Beatrix was 17. Each year, the family took long summer holidays in Scotland and, later, the English **Lake District**.

The Lake District is located in northeast England. The area is known for its lakes, forests, and mountains.

While on vacation, Beatrix and Bertram would play in the woods. There, they saw many animals. They even tamed some of the animals they found.

At home, Beatrix had many pets, including mice, rabbits, frogs, bats, and a hedgehog. Benjamin Bouncer was Beatrix's first pet rabbit. She purchased him from a pet shop in London and brought him home without her parents knowing. Peter Piper was another of Beatrix's rabbits. He was a Belgian buck rabbit and could learn tricks, such as jumping through a hoop and ringing a bell. Mrs. Tiggy-Winkle was Beatrix's pet hedgehog. She often traveled with Beatrix on the train, and she was always hungry. Spot the spaniel was the family's dog. Spot liked to travel in **carriages**. Later in life, Beatrix made pets of some of her farm animals. Pig-Wig was a black Berkshire pig that she bought from a pig farmer. She bottle-fed the pig and kept it in a basket beside her bed. She also had many farm dogs.

Beatrix studied the way her animals lived. She learned a great deal about how they behaved and the types of activities they enjoyed. Beatrix later used this information to write lively stories and draw detailed pictures.

A person's early years have a strong influence on his or her future. Parents, teachers, and friends can have a large impact on how a person thinks, feels, and behaves. These effects are strong enough to last throughout childhood, and often a person's lifetime.

In order to write about a person's early life, biographers must find answers to the following questions.

1 Where and when was the person born?

2 What is known about the person's family and friends?

3 Did the person grow up in unusual circumstances?

🖐 Beatrix Potter later wrote a book called *The Tale of Mrs. Tiggy-Winkle*. The book's main character is a hedgehog who does the laundry for other characters in the book.

Growing Up

Beatrix Potter's parents were very **protective** of their daughter. For this reason, she was homeschooled. Miss Hammond, one of Beatrix's governesses, encouraged Beatrix to draw and to write stories. She often took Beatrix to the Natural History Museum to study.

By eight years of age, Beatrix was drawing the plants and animals she saw in books and at the museum. A few years later, her parents hired an art teacher to help improve Beatrix's talents. Between 1878 and 1883, Beatrix took private art lessons from Miss Cameron. She taught the young girl how to draw **freehand** and paint using watercolors.

"I remember I used to half believe and wholly play with fairies when I was a child."
—*Beatrix Potter*

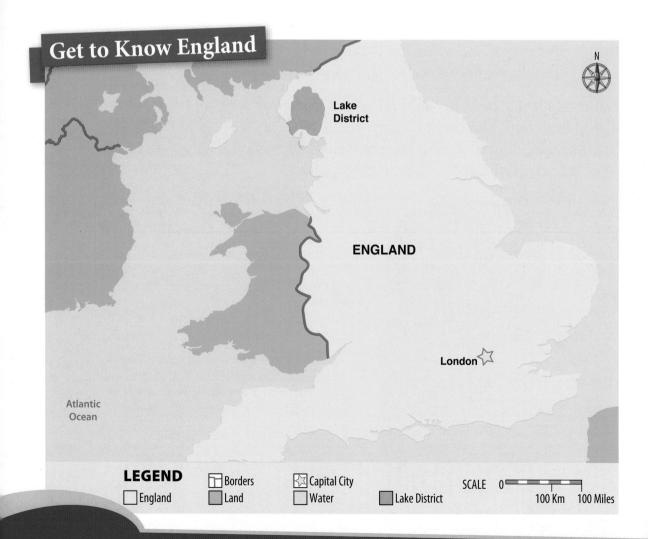

Get to Know England

N

Lake District

ENGLAND

London

Atlantic Ocean

LEGEND

☐ England   🔲 Borders   ⭐ Capital City
🔲 Land   ☐ Water   🔲 Lake District

SCALE 0 ▭▭▭ 100 Km   100 Miles

Following her time with Miss Cameron, Beatrix took 12 lessons in oil painting. However, Beatrix preferred painting with watercolors and drawing and soon stopped oil painting.

When she was 15 years old, Beatrix attended art classes at the Science and Art Department of the Committee of Council on Education. She learned to draw models and paint flowers, among other things. She later received an Art Student's Certificate for her work.

It was about this time that Beatrix began writing in a journal. She wrote in a secret code using very tiny print. Only Beatrix knew how to read the text. She continued writing in this way until she was 31. No one knows why Beatrix chose to write in code, and the code was not broken until many years after her death.

✎ In 1881, the Natural History Museum of South Kensington officially opened its doors to the public.

Writing About
Growing Up

Some people know what they want to achieve in life from a very young age. Others do not decide until much later. In any case, it is important for biographers to discuss when and how their subjects make these decisions. Using the information they collect, biographers try to answer the following questions about their subjects' paths in life.

1 Who had the most influence on the person?

2 Did he or she receive assistance from others?

3 Did the person have a positive attitude?

Developing Skills

In 1893, Beatrix began writing tales of her animal friends in letters to Noel Moore. Noel was the child of one of Beatrix's former governesses. Noel became ill when he was five years old. Beatrix made up stories and drawings to entertain him. In one letter, she wrote the story of Peter Rabbit, along with pictures.

"Believe there is a great power silently working all things for good…"
—*Beatrix Potter*

By this time, Beatrix was earning some money by writing and drawing greeting cards and book illustrations. In 1890, she earned a small fee for illustrations that she sent to the German card company Hildesheimer & Faulkner. The company asked Beatrix to send more. Three years later, Hildesheimer & Faulkner **commissioned** Beatrix to illustrate a book of children's verses, called *A Happy Pair*, by Frederic E. Weatherly.

During the 1890s, Beatrix was very interested in plants. She lived near the Natural History Museum and often went to the museum to learn about different kinds of **fungi**. She spent many hours drawing fungi and painting them in watercolor. Beatrix even wrote **theories** about lichens and mold spores.

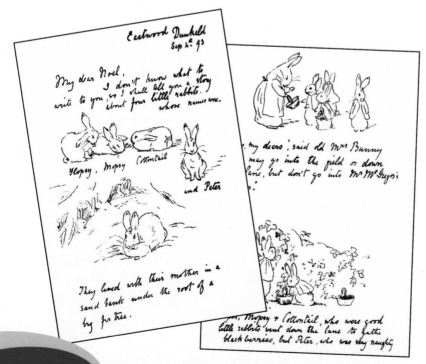

Beatrix's letters to Noel became the basis for many of her books.

When Beatrix was nearly 30 years old, she wrote a report about fungi that included detailed illustrations. Beatrix showed her work to her uncle, Sir Henry Roscoe, who was a well-respected scientist. With his help, Beatrix took her work to the Royal Botanic Gardens, where scientific studies about plants take place. The director and other scientists at the gardens thought Beatrix was too young and uneducated to understand what she was drawing. They rejected her work.

Beatrix continued to write about her theories, and her uncle took the writings to meetings at the Linnean Society of London, a group that reviews scientific evidence. At this time, women were not allowed to attend these meetings. Beatrix's writings were read to the group, but they felt it needed more work before it could be published.

After her studies on fungi were rejected, Beatrix began to draw pictures of her pets again. She also began to try other types of artwork, such as photography and needlework. However, she enjoyed painting over any other art form.

Writing About

Developing Skills

Every remarkable person has skills and traits that make him or her noteworthy. Some people have natural talent, while others practice diligently. For most, it is a combination of the two. One of the most important things that a biographer can do is to tell the story of how the subject developed his or her talents.

1 What was the person's education?

2 What was the person's first job or work experience?

3 What obstacles did the person overcome?

The Royal Botanic Gardens are sometimes called Kew Gardens. They are located in a part of London, England called Kew. The gardens were founded in 1759 and feature more than 30,000 different types of plants.

Timeline of Beatrix Potter

1866
Helen Beatrix Potter is born on July 28, in Bolton Gardens, South Kensington, London.

1881
Beatrix develops a secret code, which she uses to write journal entries.

1885
Beatrix brings home her first pet rabbit, which she names Benjamin Bouncer.

1901
Beatrix privately publishes *The Tale of Peter Rabbit*.

1895
A series of Beatrix's drawings titled *A Frog he would a-fishing go* are purchased for use in a children's book.

1890
She sells drawings of her rabbit to Hildesheimer & Faulkner to be used in cards and a book of rhymes.

1905
Beatrix becomes engaged to Norman Warne. He dies soon after.

1905
Beatrix uses her earnings to buy Hill Top, a farm in Sawrey, Lancashire.

1943
Beatrix Potter dies on December 22, in Sawrey, Lancashire.

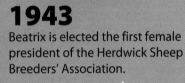

1943
Beatrix is elected the first female president of the Herdwick Sheep Breeders' Association.

1921
The first French edition of *The Tale of Peter Rabbit* is published.

1913
Beatrix marries William Heelis.

Early Achievements

Beatrix Potter did not realize her own talents until she began telling her stories to children. Aside from *The Tale of Peter Rabbit*, Beatrix wrote *The Tailor of Gloucester, The Tale of Squirrel Nutkin,* and others in letters to her governess's children. The children enjoyed Beatrix's stories, which made her think about publishing her books.

"Most people, after one success, are so cringingly afraid of doing less well that they rub all the edge off their subsequent work."
—*Beatrix Potter*

By the early 1900s, Beatrix was a successful writer and illustrator. She had found a company to publish her books. Beatrix worked closely with her editor, Norman Warne, one of the three brothers who ran the company. Norman became a dear friend, and the two wrote to each other often.

📖 Some of Beatrix's original illustrations are held in London's Tate gallery.

In 1905, Beatrix received a letter from Norman asking her to marry him. Beatrix was excited about their wedding, but she and Norman never married. He died of an illness soon after their engagement.

During this time, Beatrix had been caring for her aging parents. She had never moved out of her parents' home, but she decided to use the money she made from her books to buy a farm, called Hill Top, in the Lake District. Though she did not live at the farm right away, Beatrix visited often. In 1912, Beatrix accepted a marriage proposal from her **solicitor**, William Heelis. The two were married the following year.

Beatrix set many of her stories at her farm, Hill Top.

Tricks of the Trade

Beatrix Potter had to practice writing and drawing to perfect her skills. She had a great imagination, but she struggled to get published. Still, she kept writing and drawing until other people began to take notice of her work. Writers use many techniques to help them tell stories well. Here are some tips that young writers can use to create great stories.

Find Inspiration

Good writers are excited about their subjects. Think about what excites or interests you. It could be a person, an activity, a place, or a dream you have had. Create a list of topics you would enjoy writing about. Describe each topic as if you were telling a story about it. Try to develop a story from these notes.

Beatrix developed her children's books, including *The Tale of Jemima Puddle-Duck*, from her interest in animals.

Read

Reading other writers' stories can help you become a better writer. Their stories can help you learn new words, get ideas, and become more knowledgeable about different subjects. Beatrix Potter enjoyed reading books about nature. For her tenth birthday, Beatrix received a book called *Birds Drawn from Nature*, and she became inspired to draw and write about this subject. Visit your local library or educational websites to read about any subject that interests you.

Be Creative

Do not let boundaries limit your creativity. Beatrix Potter had a broad imagination, and she put her ideas into stories and drawings. Try to illustrate your own story. Develop unusual characters for your stories, such as a talking horse. Being creative will make your stories original. They will stand out from stories written by other writers.

Practice

It takes most writers a long time to perfect their skills. A good way to develop writing skills is to read, take writing classes, and to practice writing. Try writing in a journal every day. This will help you record any ideas that you might have. You can read your journal a year later to see how much your writing has improved.

Journals are ideal for jotting down notes and ideas about possible stories.

Remarkable Books

Beatrix Potter wrote a total of 23 books in her lifetime. Here are some of her most popular tales.

The Tale of Peter Rabbit

The Tale of Peter Rabbit has sold more than 40 million copies around the world. It was the first title in a series of illustrated books. In this book, Peter Rabbit and his three sisters, Mopsy, Flopsy and Cotton-tail, live with their mother under a large fir tree. Peter likes to get into mischief. He goes into Mr. McGregor's garden and eats some of Mr. McGregor's vegetables. Mr. McGregor discovers what Peter has done and chases him through the garden. Peter loses his shoes and gets tangled in some netting. He escapes just as Mr. McGregor is about to catch him.

Peter runs to the gardening shed and hides in a watering can. Mr. McGregor discovers the hiding place when Peter sneezes. Peter keeps on running from Mr. McGregor and finally makes it home safely. Mr. McGregor makes a scarecrow out of the clothes that Peter Rabbit lost while running away from him. Peter Rabbit does not feel well at dinner, and his mother sends him to bed early with some medicine.

The Tale of Squirrel Nutkin

The Tale of Squirrel Nutkin is about a little red squirrel who has a large tail. Nutkin goes to gather some nuts on Owl Island with a group of squirrels. Instead of collecting nuts with the others, Nutkin spends all of his time playing. For six days straight, all of the squirrels go to collect nuts on the island, while Nutkin plays or gets into mischief. Every time the squirrels visit the island, they give gifts to Old Brown, the owl that lives there. When Nutkin sees the owl, he dances and sings riddles. Old Brown gets annoyed with Nutkin and captures him. Nutkin escapes, but he loses most of his large, bushy tail.

The Tale of Benjamin Bunny

Benjamin Bunny appears in a few Beatrix Potter books, including *The Tale of the Flopsy Bunnies* and *The Tale of Mr. Tod*. In *The Tale of Benjamin Bunny*, Benjamin and his cousin Peter Rabbit search through Mr. McGregor's garden to try to find the clothes that Peter lost in *The Tale of Peter Rabbit*. This time, Mr. McGregor has gone out with Mrs. McGregor. Benjamin and Peter find the clothes and gather onions from the garden. As they try to leave, Benjamin and Peter spot a cat at the garden gate. The pair are afraid that the cat will hurt them, so they hide under a basket.

Benjamin Bunny's father attacks the cat and rescues Benjamin and Peter. They return home, and Peter Rabbit gives his mother the onions. She forgives him for losing his clothes.

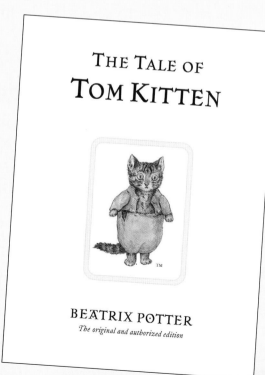

The Tailor of Gloucester

The Tailor of Gloucester is about a poor tailor who has a cat and several mice living in his shop. The tailor has many scrap pieces of material that he cannot use, and the mice make themselves clothing from the scraps. The tailor sends his cat, Simpkin, to get him some food and a piece of cherry-colored silk thread. The thread is for a coat that the tailor is making for the mayor's wedding on Christmas morning. While Simpkin is shopping, the tailor lets the mice out from where the cat has trapped them. When Simpkin returns, he finds all of the mice are missing. He gets angry and hides the thread. The tailor becomes ill, so the mice finish making the mayor's coat for him.

The Tale of Tom Kitten

This is a story about three little kittens. Tabitha Twitchit is the mother of these mischievous kittens. One day, Tabitha finds out that guests are coming to visit her. She gathers her children together to wash them and dress them in clean clothes. She tells the kittens that they can play outside if they promise to keep clean. The kittens promptly go outside, get dirty, and lose all of their clothes to some ducks. When the kittens return home, their mother is very angry. She hides them upstairs and tells her guests that the kittens have the measles.

From Big Ideas to Books

At first, it was difficult for Beatrix to get her books published. It was hard for women at this time to be taken seriously as writers and artists. After Beatrix's paper on fungi was rejected, she was unsure if she should continue writing.

As a young woman, Beatrix's uncle, Sir Henry Roscoe, urged her to try to sell her art. Beatrix made six drawings of Benjamin Bouncer for Christmas cards. Her brother, Bertram, brought them to Hildesheimer & Faulkner. They liked what they saw and sent Beatrix a small check. They also asked her to send more drawings.

> "I cannot rest, I must draw, however poor the result, and when I have a bad time come over me it is a stronger desire than ever."
> —Beatrix Potter

Later, a family friend, Canon Rawnsley, encouraged Beatrix to have her works published. Canon Rawnsley was a published author who was very interested in Beatrix's drawings. He suggested that Beatrix give her sample of *The Tale of Peter Rabbit* to a publishing company called Frederick Warne & Co. They rejected her book, so Beatrix decided to make her own version.

The Publishing Process

Publishing companies receive hundreds of **manuscripts** from authors each year. Only a few manuscripts become books. Publishers must be sure that a manuscript will sell many copies. As a result, publishers reject most of the manuscripts they receive. Once a manuscript has been accepted, it goes through

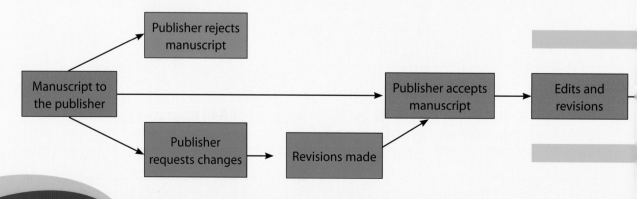

Beatrix approached a printer, and in 1901, 250 copies of her little book were made. Beatrix sold copies of the book to her friends and relatives. She sent a copy of her book to Frederick Warne & Co. They decided to publish a new version of the book. This version would have color pictures instead of black and white. Beatrix set to work redrawing the pictures in color and adding some new ones. When she was done, Frederick Warne & Co. printed 8,000 copies of the new *The Tale of Peter Rabbit*.

Beatrix Potter's books continue to be popular. Companies have developed other products, such as dishes and tablecloths, that feature her animal characters.

Beatrix wrote *The Tailor of Gloucester* one year later. These first two books sold well. In 1903, *The Tale of Squirrel Nutkin* was published, and it was a huge success. Beatrix continued to generate ideas for new books. She went on to publish another 20 books over the next 10 years.

many stages before it is published. Often, authors change their work to follow an editor's suggestions. Once the book is published, some authors receive royalties. This is money based on book sales.

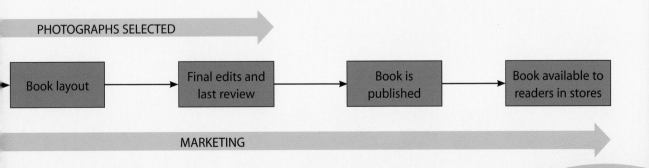

PHOTOGRAPHS SELECTED

Book layout → Final edits and last review → Book is published → Book available to readers in stores

MARKETING

Beatrix Potter Today

Beatrix Potter lived with her parents until she wed in 1913. However, she had bought Hill Top in 1905. When she was not caring for her parents, Beatrix spent a great deal of time farming and sheep herding at the farm. Four years later, she bought more land called Castle Farm.

After Beatrix and William Heelis wed, Beatrix spent little time writing. Instead, she focused on sheep farming. She became an award-winning Herdwick sheep breeder and was elected the first female president of the Herdwick Sheep Breeders' Association.

Beatrix Potter became an active member of her community. She took a special interest in preserving the beauty of the Lake District.

Sawrey is actually two villages called Near Sawrey and Far Sawrey. Beatrix Potter lived in Near Sawrey.

During World War I, Beatrix's publisher fell on hard times. To help the company earn more money, Beatrix published another children's book called *Appley Dapply's Nursery Rhymes*, as well as two painting activity books. After this time, Beatrix published only a few more books, including the little book *The Tale of Little Pig Robinson*, which was printed in 1930. The last book published during Beatrix's lifetime was *Sister Anne* in 1932. She did not illustrate the book, and it was only sold in the United States.

By the late 1930s, Beatrix was in poor health. She died in 1943, at Castle Farm in Sawrey. She left most of her property to the National Trust. This is a charity that protects more than 300 historic houses and gardens, as well as many mills, monuments, forests, farms, and castles. Beatrix Potter left Hill Top and about 4,000 acres of land to the Trust.

Writing About the Person Today

The biography of any living person is an ongoing story. People have new ideas, start new projects, and deal with challenges. For their work to be meaningful, biographers must include up-to-date information about their subjects. Through research, biographers try to answer the following questions.

1 Has the person received awards or recognition for accomplishments?

2 What is the person's life's work?

3 How have the person's accomplishments served others?

Fan Information

Today, Beatrix Potter fans can remember the writer and artist by visiting Hill Top. Hill Top has been restored to look exactly as it did when Beatrix lived there. The former offices of William Heelis in Hawkshead now house the Beatrix Potter Gallery, where some of Beatrix's letters and drawings are on display.

Beatrix's fans can visit the World of Beatrix Potter Attraction in Bowness-on-Windermere in the Lake District, England. Here, visitors can walk through life-like scenes from all 23 tales by Beatrix Potter. The attraction features short films and exhibits about Beatrix's life, and visitors can have tea with Peter Rabbit.

Many of Beatrix Potter's works have been stored with the National Trust or in museums. The National Trust has many first edition copies of her books and more than 700 watercolors and ink drawings. It also has furniture from Hill Top and copies of some of Beatrix's manuscripts and her personal items, including a set of place mats that Beatrix hand painted. The Warne Archive of Beatrix's letters, artwork, and more is housed at the Victoria and Albert Museum in London, England.

The World of Beatrix Potter Attraction is the only Beatrix Potter-themed attraction in Europe.

Since Beatrix's death, several movies and plays have been made about her books and her life. In 1971, a film called *The Tales of Beatrix Potter* used ballet dancers and music to tell many of Beatrix's stories. In 1982, *The Tale of Beatrix Potter*, a fact-based movie about the writer's life, was released. Another movie, *Miss Potter*, was released in 2006. It is a romantic movie about Beatrix's life with Norman.

A number of books have been written about Beatrix Potter. Linda Lear wrote *Beatrix Potter: A Life in Nature*. This biography was published in 2006. Fans can learn about Beatrix Potter's life by reading her diary, *The Journal of Beatrix Potter, 1881-1897*, which was published in 1966. The diary includes a great deal of information about Beatrix's family. *Beatrix Potter: Artist, Storyteller & Countrywoman* by Judy Taylor is another great source for information about Beatrix.

In the movie *Miss Potter*, Renée Zellweger played Beatrix Potter, and Ewan McGregor took on the role of Norman Warne.

Write a Biography

All of the parts of a biography work together to tell the story of a person's life. Find out how these elements combine by writing a biography. Begin by choosing a person whose story fascinates you. You will have to research the person's life by using library books and reliable websites. You can also e-mail the person or write him or her a letter. The person might agree to answer your questions directly.

Use a concept web, such as the one below, to guide you in writing the biography. Answer each of the questions listed using the information you have gathered. Each heading on the concept web will form an important part of the person's story.

Parts of a Biography

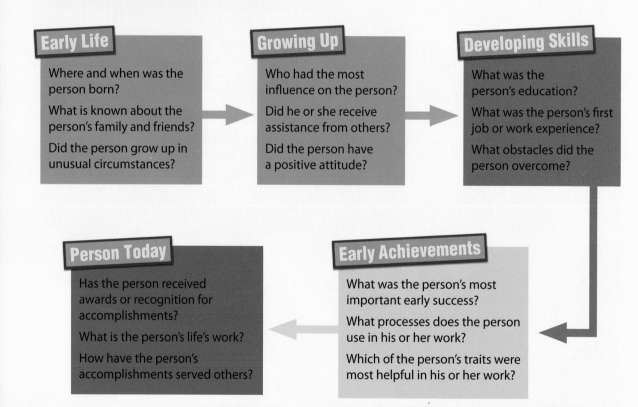

Early Life

Where and when was the person born?

What is known about the person's family and friends?

Did the person grow up in unusual circumstances?

Growing Up

Who had the most influence on the person?

Did he or she receive assistance from others?

Did the person have a positive attitude?

Developing Skills

What was the person's education?

What was the person's first job or work experience?

What obstacles did the person overcome?

Person Today

Has the person received awards or recognition for accomplishments?

What is the person's life's work?

How have the person's accomplishments served others?

Early Achievements

What was the person's most important early success?

What processes does the person use in his or her work?

Which of the person's traits were most helpful in his or her work?

Test Yourself

1 How many tales did Beatrix Potter write?

2 What did Beatrix study at the Natural History Museum?

3 Who encouraged Beatrix to have her books published?

4 How did Beatrix write in her secret diary?

5 Which organizations now keep many of Beatrix's original pieces?

6 What company first published Beatrix's drawings?

7 When was Beatrix's last little book published?

8 What was the first book that Beatrix published?

9 What was the name of the first farm Beatrix bought?

10 When did Beatrix die?

ANSWERS

1. She wrote 23 tales. 2. She studied fungi. 3. Canon Rawnsley encouraged Beatrix. 4. She wrote in a secret code that only she could understand. 5. The National Trust, and the Warne Archive, at the Victoria and Albert Museum, have many of her works. 6. Hildesheimer & Faulkner published A Happy Pair. 7. The last little book was published in 1930. 8. The Tale of Peter Rabbit was the first book she published. 9. Beatrix's first farm was Hill Top. 10. Beatrix died in 1943.

Writing Terms

This glossary will introduce you to some of the main terms in the field of writing. Understanding these common writing terms will allow you to discuss your ideas about books and writing with others.

action: the moving events of a work of fiction

antagonist: the person in the story who opposes the main character

autobiography: a history of a person's life written by that person

biography: a written account of another person's life

character: a person in a story, poem, or play

climax: the most exciting moment or turning point in a story

episode: a short piece of action, or scene, in a story

fiction: stories about characters and events that are not real

foreshadow: hinting at something that is going to happen later in the book

imagery: a written description of a thing or idea that brings an image to mind

narrator: the speaker of the story who relates the events

nonfiction: writing that deals with real people and events

novel: published writing of considerable length that portrays characters within a story

plot: the order of events in a work of fiction

protagonist: the leading character of a story; often a likable character

resolution: the end of the story, when the conflict is settled

scene: a single episode in a story

setting: the place and time in which a work of fiction occurs

theme: an idea that runs throughout a work of fiction

Key Words

carriages: vehicles that have four wheels and are pulled by horses

commissioned: to be hired by a company or person and paid to do specific work

freehand: to draw without the aid of tools, such as a ruler

fungi: a spongy, abnormal plant-like organism, such as yeast, mold, and mushrooms

governesses: women that are hired to raise and teach a child

Lake District: England's largest national park

manuscripts: original texts of an author's work

protective: very caring and guarding

solicitor: a lawyer who deals with certain legal matters

theories: ideas used to explain something

Index

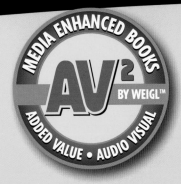

Log on to www.av2books.com

AV[2] by Weigl brings you media enhanced books that support active learning. Go to www.av2books.com, and enter the special code found on page 2 of this book. You will gain access to enriched and enhanced content that supplements and complements this book. Content includes video, audio, weblinks, quizzes, a slide show, and activities.

AV[2] Online Navigation

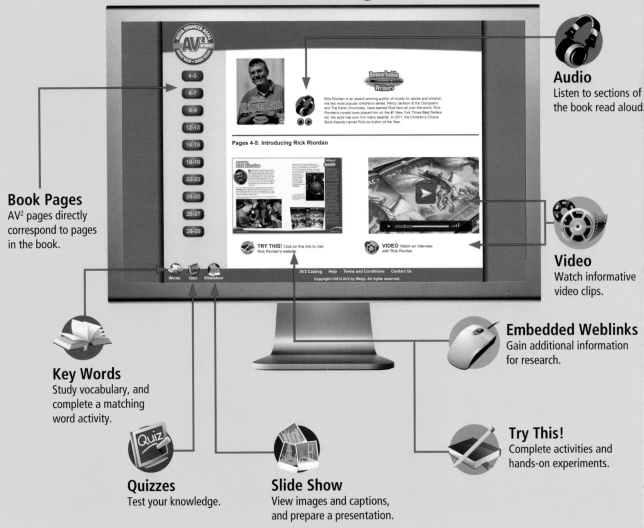

Audio
Listen to sections of the book read aloud.

Book Pages
AV[2] pages directly correspond to pages in the book.

Video
Watch informative video clips.

Key Words
Study vocabulary, and complete a matching word activity.

Embedded Weblinks
Gain additional information for research.

Try This!
Complete activities and hands-on experiments.

Quizzes
Test your knowledge.

Slide Show
View images and captions, and prepare a presentation.

AV[2] was built to bridge the gap between print and digital. We encourage you to tell us what you like and what you want to see in the future.

Sign up to be an AV[2] Ambassador at www.av2books.com/ambassador.